Slow Down to Scale Up!

*Business Owners, Entrepreneurs, CEOs,
and Leaders: Learn to Unleash Your
Maximum Potential, Master Peace of
Mind, and Achieve More Each Day*

Aisling Nestor

Orla Kelly Publishing
27 Kilbrody,
Mount Oval,
Rochestown,
Cork,
Ireland.

Dedication

I would like to dedicate this book to my cousin Bridie. She is my rock and always supports and encourages me when I have outrageous ideas about what I want to create next in my business and life. She believes in me and constantly encourages and motivates me to be and do even more. Everyone needs a Bridie in their life!

Thank you, Bridie x

Contents

Who is this book for?

Hello, I am Aisling Nestor and I've got your back. I can say that is my hallmark throughout my career. No matter who you are or where you work, I have your back.

What people say about everything and anything that I do is: "She gave it her all."

At 6 years of age, I began my love and joy for playing the piano and the kind of dancing that made my body feel alive; I have never lost these feelings. I gave that my all and that is how I live my life to date.

My background is in Mental Health Nursing - one of the most challenging areas of nursing that anyone can practice. And I gave it my all for the entire time that I worked there. I was known for my reliability, empathy, and capabilities. Each client could count on me. I had their back. I was their advocate. No matter who you were if you needed support; I was there. I was a great communicator, and I learned how to deal with conflicts that were often intense.

Now, I work with business owners, entrepreneurs, CEO's, and other leaders who are open and vulnerable and need help to kickstart their lives and their businesses.

I work with people who thrive on life's challenges. Ironically, the problem with thriving on challenges is that sometimes it feels like a drug that you can never quite get enough of.

I work with people who spend a lot of time trying to avoid conflict. I teach them not to get mired in conflict by remaining so grounded and solid that people know they can trust you because you have their back.

If you need people to know how much they can count on you, you can count on me. And you and I should have a conversation.

I promise to show up 100% at every conversation that we have. To hide nothing and hold nothing back. I will always be honest with what I see and hear. I will call you out on your excuses!

How I work

I work with business owners, entrepreneurs, CEOs, and leaders who have experience doing the same thing over and over and are not getting the results they want, despite the success they have already created in their lives.

My approach focuses on five key areas:

Vision

New Skill Development

Managing complex challenges and decisions

Developing emotional intelligence and

Spiritual growth

Combined with my critical insights and expertise in human behaviour and business development, I will help you find and resolve the vulnerabilities in your business and life, while helping you to slow down and scale up. You will learn to live the life of your dreams and build your business with peace of mind, and a feeling of freedom to enjoy a new way of living and operating your business.

Would you be interested in a business and life where you can find greater peace of mind, freedom, time, revenue, and influence in your industry?

I want you to allow yourself to really sit with this question and allow yourself to imagine the opportunities and possibilities this will provide you in your business and life.

The key issues I see over and over in my clients are the following:

- Health Concerns.

- Gold Medal Depression.

- Loss of Purpose.

- Identity Crisis.

- Lack of Respect from Others.

- Social Isolation.

- Envy towards others' successes, and

- Stress.

I create a bespoke coaching programme for each client I work with to meet their individual needs, while helping them to achieve their desired business and life goals.

I now want to share a powerful short story with you.

There's A Hole In My Sidewalk

Autobiography in Five Short Chapters
(Portia Nelson, 1977)

I.

I walk down the street. There is a deep hole in the sidewalk. I fall in. I am lost…. I am helpless. It isn't my fault. It takes forever to find a way out.

II.

I walk down the same street. There is a deep hole in the sidewalk. I pretend that I don't see it. I fall in again. I can't believe I am in this same place. But it isn't my fault. It still takes a long time to get out.

III.

I walk down the same street. There is a deep hole in the sidewalk. I see it there. I still fall in… it's a habit…. but, my eyes are open. I know where I am. It is *my* fault. I get out immediately.

IV.

I walk down the same street. There is a deep hole in the sidewalk. I walk around it.

V.

I walk down a different street.

Which stage are you at? Are you still falling into those potholes, or have you learned a better way of doing things?

I will now take you through one of the processes that I use with my clients to help them slow down and scale up.

To find the greatest value from the following exercises, I invite you to sit back with a cup of tea or beverage of your choice, slow down and discover new information about yourself that you can use to scale up your life and business.

Please note, while reading and filling in the following workbook, you may observe that some sections overlap; that is fine.. It will all come together when you have completed it. You will also realise how important each question and section is. They are all interwoven- just like Business and Life.

If you prefer not to write in the workbook, please write in your journal or notebook.

Meeting Minster of Health-Mary Butler

Slow Down to Scale Up
Workbook

1

Lacking Focus

You need a crystal-clear vision

You can only know where to focus and what to focus on when you discover where you are headed, and why you are heading there!

Allow yourself to slow down to answer the following questions to find your crystal-clear vision. This is the first step that you will take to scale up your life and business.

You then can focus on your day-to-day tasks and the bigger legacy you want to create.

This part of the process takes time. So, allow yourself the time that you need. After all, this is your future that you are about to create.

What's not in my life that I want and need?

How can I make my future bigger than my past?

What's not in my business that I want and need?

What do I want my life and business to look and feel like in 5 years' time?

How does it feel when I allow myself to think about it?

What is stopping me from having all of my 5-year goals right now?

What is really stopping me from having all of that right now? It's time to be honest with yourself!

What is stopping me from making these changes?

What is it costing me to not make these changes?

What have I tried already to make this vision happen?

What do I need to make this vision happen?

On a scale of 1-10 how committed am I to taking the necessary steps to make my vision happen?

If you are a 7 or under, you are not committed enough. If 8 or over, you are already committed to your future life and business goals.

Am I ready, willing and able?

Action: What action can I take today to help start to make my vision a reality?

Small hinges swing big doors - small actions create big results - Take a small step and see the big impact it can have on your business and life.

Testimonial:

Clare McKenna - Broadcaster & Health Coach

"Aisling was a guest on my radio show, sharing her story of burnout and the lessons she learned. When she suggested some of her coaching sessions, I wasn't sure what to expect, but from the very first one, she had me sussed and reframed so many of my subconscious thought patterns. From then, she really helped me build a new approach to how I work, from valuing my time, learning to say no, and knowing my worth. She has a killer combination of a sweet and gentle personality but razor-sharp intuition and lots of knowledge to help you progress on your path and go further."

2

Not seeing results fast enough

You Need to Slow Down to Speed Up

Yes, I know, this sounds like the biggest contradiction ever! I challenge you to try this. What have you got to lose?

When you are switched on all the time, whether mentally and/or physically, you probably find yourself not able to:

Fully focus.

Have full clarity.

Feel energised.

Make confident decisions.

Be consistent with your actions.

Be creative.

When you learn to slow down, you actually speed up in all these areas! Go on, have the courage to try something different. Doing what you always do is no longer getting you the desired results.

I want to inform you of the definition of insanity-it's doign the same thing over and over and expecting a different result.

If this is you, please don't let yourself be in this place any longer.

Imagine you have learned to slow down. What can now happen in your life and business?

What impact will slowing down have on you, your life and your business?

How does it feel to think about those possibilities and opportunities?

 Action: What can you do today to slow down?

Small hinges swing big doors - small actions create big results -Take a small step and see the big impact it can have on your business and life.

Testimonial:

Orla Kelly - Owner of Orla Kelly Publishing

"Before I spoke to Aisling, my biggest challenge was that I was constantly juggling workload, and things were manic. I was exhausted and worked longer hours. With Aisling's insights, she helped me raise awareness of what I was and wasn't doing and suggested changes I could implement. Not just the changes she recommended but how she helped me see how I was operating. I had a major breakthrough in my realisation, and these changes are now paying off.

Aisling is very intuitive and listens to what you say but also tunes into what lies underneath, even at a level you may not know. She is open and genuinely cares. I would recommend that anyone speak to Aisling. You never know where that conversation will lead and how your life will change for the better as a result. Thank you, Aisling!"

3

Not seeing the same results you are usually capable of achieving

Imagine using your usual skillset to create your results, but that skillset has stopped having the same impact! This is an extremely frustrating place to find yourself in.

In a nutshell, what has happened is: **Your Biggest Strength Is Now Your Biggest Weakness!**

Imagine finding hidden skills inside of you that will help you to create new and even bigger results.

Begin by listing your skills/strengths below.

What is the dark side/weakness to your strengths?

How is this dark side impacting your life and your business?

Which insights have you just discovered about yourself?

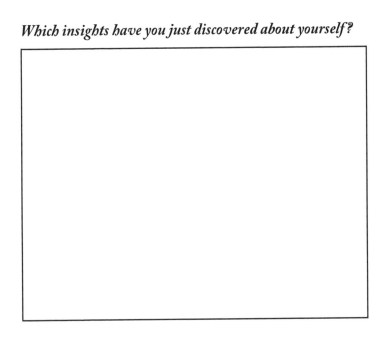

 Action: Reflect on how your greatest strengths, when overused, have a negative impact, and how this is interfering with your ability to slow down and scale up.

Small hinges swing big doors - small actions create big results -Take a small step and see the big impact it can have on your business and life.

Testimonial:

Sarah Jane Foster - SJF Productions

"Aisling is a true professional. I am honoured to have done my business coaching with her. She gave me so much confidence and clarity for my business. She is really passionate and genuine about what she does. I would highly recommend Aisling."

4

**Life and Business are Chaotic.
Everything is a priority that
needs to be done now!**

Task and Time Management are now going to be your best friends!

I help clients identify the 20% of tasks that will generate 80% of their revenue. This, in turn, helps my clients gain clarity and control over their hours, days and weeks. The result? Savouring a sense of calmness, peace of mind and lots of free time- the dream life and dream business life.

To help you discover the 20% of tasks that generate 80% of your revenue, answer these questions:

1. What are the top 3 – 5 tasks that generate revenue in your business?

2. Which tasks have to be completed today? Or have an urgent deadline?

3. Which tasks can wait until tomorrow or next week?

4. What is stopping you from focusing almost exclusively on your priority tasks?

 Action: How can you ensure that you are doing the 20% of tasks each day that generate 80% of your revenue?

Small hinges swing big doors - small actions create big results - Take a small step and see the big impact it can have on your business and life.

Testimonial:

Tina Brigley - Transformational Life Coach

"Aisling is a coach who is committed to her own growth as much as her client's growth. She is the real deal. Her knowledge and experience allow her to see the gaps her clients can't see. She has a keen ability to help businesses increase their revenue and develop their team. I wouldn't hesitate to recommend her."

3. Do these thoughts and stories serve you in creating the life and business of your dreams?

Action: Over the next week, I want you to become aware of how often you have these negative thoughts and old, limiting stories. I invite you to record when and where these beliefs and stories appear in your life and business. You will be surprised to see where and how often they appear! Observe what happens when you gain awareness of your negative thoughts and old limiting stories.

Small hinges swing big doors - small actions create big results - Take a small step and see the big impact it can have in your business and life.

Decisions are best made when aligned with what is really important to you, along with your crystal-clear vision (Step 1).

Making decisions that align with your values is essential, whether making decisions in your life or business, even complex decisions. This is not always easy, but this approach ensures you are true to yourself in both life and career.

You can identify some of your values by answering the following questions:

What is important to you? (freedom, family, fun, rest, play)

When you have written down 10 values, I want you to rate them. How well are you honouring your values on a scale of 1-10 (10 being the best)? Explain how you can honour each value more.

Value	Score	How can I honour this value more?

 Action: Choose a way to start honouring your values in life and business.

Small hinges swing big doors - small actions create big results - Take a small step and see the big impact it can have on your business and life.

Testimonial:

Sam Salem (Retail Store Manager)

Trying to balance life, work and family was like trying to juggle when all the balls constantly changing weight week to week. It felt as if some part needed the majority of my focus and was cutting into work or home life. It was a challenge to separate work and home mentally, sometimes it worked great and other times one or the other was nearly all consuming. My mind was constantly in both work and home mode all day which led to me not being able to fully commit to either.

Currently, I have a fantastic balance where I can be fully present at home and at work. I feel like whether it's work or home they get me complete and all in. My mind is so much quieter and calmer that I can function immensely better than before.

What has changed in essence is Me. Aisling has helped me greatly to improve my mindset, my self-worth, confidence, my priorities to name but a few. I now set tasks and make decisions virtually stress free and instantly so no more internal debate for days on a decision. Which has freed my mind up to be very productive. I leave work at work and any stresses or negativity doesn't come home with me.

I would highly encourage anyone if they have the opportunity to work with Aisling. Aisling doesn't have a magic pill to change you but rather helps you develop skills to improve yourself and get you closer and closer to where you want to be.

Do You Want to Work with Aisling?

Each of us has the ability to create the life and business of our dreams.

Looking at everything I have shared with you, up to this point and at your honest answers to each part's questions, where do you see yourself?

Select the option below that most represents your thinking on where you currently are at:

1. You are not ready to make changes for whatever reason. And that is ok. I wish you all the best. Change will happen when you are ready, and I am here when you are ready to start making those changes.

2. The information in this book is all you need to make the necessary changes in your life and business. If this is you, I congratulate you and wish you all the best in your journey. I am thrilled that I was able to guide you to this place. Please send me an email to share this information with me. I mean it; I would love to hear about your success.

3. You are ready to say yes to yourself and your business and know you will get there faster working with Aisling. If so, contact me today, and we will discuss how to make this happen!

4. You are on the fence. (PTO if this is where you currently are.)

If you are on the fence about working with me, ask yourself the following questions:

Where will my business be in a year's time if I make no changes? How will I feel?

What is it costing me to not make the necessary changes?

What can I lose by investing in my business and myself?

What can be gained by investing in my business and myself?

What would be different if I invested in my business and myself?

How does that make me feel?

Go back to page 46 and see what score you give yourself now.

Work with Aisling

Don't waste your precious resources doing the same thing repeatedly, expecting different results. Reach out, and let's work on moving you forward. Feel free to contact me for a chat to see how I can help you.

If you are ready to make positive changes in your life and your business, please email me at aislingcbc@gmail.com or call me on +353 87 9383214.

Milton Keynes UK
Ingram Content Group UK Ltd.
UKHW021146100324
438949UK00008B/101